to
nd
a
end

For Dr Kris Zegocki, Clinical Nurse Specialist Karen Bennett
and all the amazing NHS staff at Whipps Cross Hospital and
St. Bart's Hospital, London – Thank You! ~ K N

For Farheen, Rachel and Emilie. Thank you for the
countless years of love and support!
~ C A

A STUDIO PRESS BOOK

First published in the UK in 2021 by Studio Press,
an imprint of Bonnier Books UK,
The Plaza, 535 King's Road, London SW10 0SZ
Owned by Bonnier Books,
Sveavägen 56, Stockholm, Sweden

www.studiopressbooks.co.uk
www.bonnierbooks.co.uk

Text copyright © 2021 Karl Newson
Illustrations copyright © 2021 Clara Anganuzzi

1 3 5 7 9 10 8 6 4 2

ISBN 978-1-78741-771-7

FSC
www.fsc.org
MIX
Paper from
responsible sources
FSC® C104723

Edited by Frankie Jones and Ellie Rose
Designed by Verity Clark

A CIP catalogue for this book is available from the British Library
Printed and bound in China

How to Mend a Friend

Karl Newson

illustrated by

Clara Anganuzzi

STUDIO PRESS

Some friends need a great **big hug**

to help them feel well.

Some prefer to be **alone**.

Some **listen**.

Others tell ...

...the most

adventurous stories

of the times

that went before!

Some friends may not want
to talk about them anymore.

Some friends need a little help to find their smile again ...

It could be in the rising sun.

It might **be** in the rain.

Some friends like
to read a book,

and some friends
like a bath.

Some just want to watch TV,

while others need to laugh.

Some friends

have a list of things

they'd like to try to do.

Some friends will be happiest,
just to be with **you** . . .

sitting, doing nothing much,
and saying not a word.

(Sometimes just a tiny **smile**
will let them know you've heard.)

Some friends keep a diary.

Some friends write a letter.

Some will sing their favourite songs to help themselves feel better.

Some friends say a flower helps a heart that has an ache.

Some prefer an ice-cream or a homemade chocolate cake.

Some friends don't want anything ... except to feel sad.

Some friends want for all the things
they wish that they still had.

Some friends want to go back home.

Some may want to

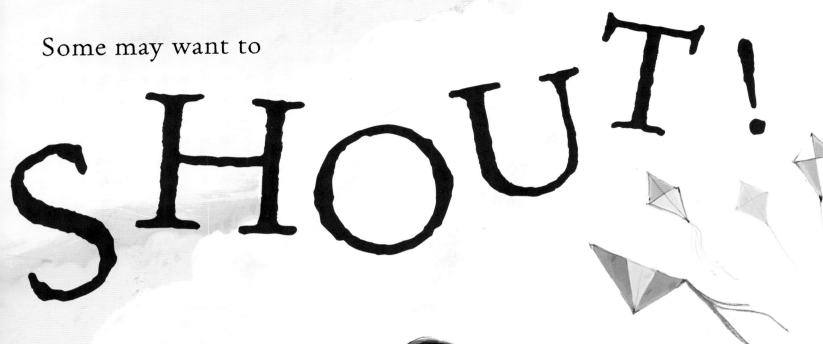

SHOUT!

Some friends want
to keep it in,

while others let it out!

Some friends like to share their hearts
to show you that they care.

Some friends like to send a note,
to let you know they're there.

Some friends will be with you,
even if they are afar.

Some friends will be
there for you,
no matter where
you are.

Some friends will grow old with you.

Some may come and go.

Some will teach you things about yourself you didn't know.

Some **friends** need a little **hug** to help them to feel good.

Some
friends
want to
run it
off . . .

around the neighbourhood.

Some friends want to fly away.

Some
friends
want
to hide.

Some **friends** might want someone else.
But, still, they'll know you tried.

And maybe, in a while,
they'll be **pleased** that you were there...

All of us are different.
Everybody.
Everywhere.

Some friends
need a lot of friends.
To help them see
things through …

You can be the greatest friend
just by being you.

This story was written in the middle of my cancer treatment, when the days were
a haze and the future was quite uncertain. Although it was one of the darker times of my life
I found myself filled with a feeling of constant love and support from all those around me,
from my partner who was there with me every single day (even when I was not there myself!),
to my doctors, nurses and all the amazing NHS staff who lifted me up and found time to get to
know me and enjoy a giggle in what were otherwise very strange and surreal days, to my family who
filled me up with support and love, and to my friends of old and new who reached out from afar
and gifted me with daily messages of support, and biscuits, and amazingly with what began as
one, but soon grew into a whole herd of elephant illustrations that I will treasure for all my days.

This story is all those feelings I experienced, wrapped up in one, and sent with a great big hug.
It's my 'Thank You' to them all for getting me through. I'd also like to say a special
thank you to Clara Anganuzzi for bringing my words to life so wonderfully, and to
the brilliant team at Studio Press for publishing me.

I hope the story helps anyone who needs it and reassures the reader
that just being 'you' is as perfect as can be.

Karl Newson